SOWING SEEDS

Essentials for
Small Community Leaders

RENEW International
Plainfield, New Jersey

NIHIL OBSTAT
Reverend Monsignor James M. Cafone, S.T.D.
Archdiocese of Newark
Censor Librorum

IMPRIMATUR
Most Reverend John J. Myers, J.C.D., D.D.
Archbishop of Newark

CONTENTS

FOREWORD

Sowing Seeds is a powerful image to describe not only the work of small Christian community leaders in the life of the Church today, but also the foundational help that this guide provides for such leaders, veteran and new. After spending considerable time reflecting on the practical wisdom offered and the invaluable skills reinforced from chapter to chapter in this Leaders' Guidebook, the image of "sowing seeds" becomes even more compelling. "In the seed lie the life and the future" (Marion Zimmer Bradley).

Like all of you, I believe passionately in God's dream for this world. I believe that this dream has much to do with our becoming one, healed of all divisions, one family of faith, one human family and one planetary family, desirous that life flourish for all in all its diversity. God's dream is big and we are small; God's dream is about fullness of life and a future full of hope. Our grasp on life is transitory and fragile; our vision of life is limited. Making all one is the work of God in Christ, who is laboring to bring it about with our cooperation. Our job is to plant seeds and water the seeds already planted.

In my own personal life, I have not experienced any more powerful way to cooperate faithfully with this dream of God than by building up small communities of faith ... one community at a time. As a Sister of St. Joseph, I have been committed to life in community for several decades. What a tremendous gift it was for me to realize early on in my religious life that community was not something reserved for members of religious congregations alone. No, community is a gospel value and a call. It is the gift and responsibility of every Christian, flowing from our baptisms. "There is no such thing as an isolated Christian," Tertullian exclaimed in the second century. Leaders of small Christian communities help provide a communal way for Christians to journey together toward fullness of life in Christ. It is a holy work; it is participation in the reaping of God's harvest.

If this Leader's Guide did no more than recommend how we as 21st century Christians might learn to listen to one another more effectively with vulnerability, acceptance, expectancy, and constancy, it would be well-worth the read, but this is only one contribution *Sowing Seeds* provides. I suspect that each leader who, like me, uses this guidebook will move back and forth in claiming the chapters that best respond to their practical questions and those that best rekindle their ministerial call to service.

For myself, I was once again inspired by how clearly the authors lead us to see the natural flow from shared faith to shared action, from transformed hearts to helping to transform our world. They provide a chapter that does indeed sound the call for us to be leaven in the world—but much more than simply sounding the call, they provide strategic steps for how we can respond to the call. The invitation to "Go and serve" is at the heart of Jesus' life and ministry and at the heart of every community gathered in Jesus' name. The dynamic movement from community to action and from action back to reflection in community provides the rhythm of the Christian journey. This guidebook helps us catch the Spirit's beat and move with it.

As someone who learned from Tom Kleissler and Mary McGuinness early on how to serve as a small Christian community leader and how to encourage others to share this significant role in the life of the community, I marvel at the clarity of their teaching and at the untiring zeal of their commitment to provide the inspiration and skills for the next generation of leaders to take up the essential work of sowing seeds. There are few people in our country, I dare say in our world, who have believed more deeply, perceived more clearly or given their lives more passionately for the promotion of small Christian communities in the life of the Church and for the sake of the world than Msgr. Tom Kleissler and Sr. Mary McGuinness, OP. Learning from them about the role of leadership in small community development is indeed to sit at the feet of the masters. Yet they have never left the ranks of learners, faithful seed-sowers themselves, which is why and how they remember and share so clearly the art and practical skills of forming leaders. The experiential knowledge contained in this guidebook is but so many seeds they sow in the waiting soil of leaders' hearts. I am confident that leaders and potential leaders of small Christian communities will find in this resource book the confidence, reassurance, skill, and inspiration they seek to serve their small community and the Church lovingly, wisely, and well.

I am so happy to have an opportunity here to thank these two small community leaders for their indefatiguable service to the world Church; to the Church and world. May we, who learn from them, respond to the grace of sowing seeds of community in our time and place. This little guide, *Sowing Seeds*, makes it possible for us, as small Christian community leaders, to make that response generously, wholeheartedly and trustingly. We can do it; God will help—so will this wonderful resource!

Catherine T. Nerney, SSJ, PhD
Associate Professor of Theology and Spirituality
Chestnut Hill College, Philadelphia, PA
President, National Association
Small Christian Communities Connection

INTRODUCTION

Sowing Seeds has grown out of RENEW International's very foundational roots—thirty years experience of successfully fostering the spiritual growth of people through the development of small Christian communities. RENEW International's history is wide and varied, yet always grounded in the Catholic tradition of leading people to holiness, to a deeper appreciation and sharing of their faith through reflection on Scripture, and to connect faith with their daily lives, that is, being Good News for others.

RENEW International began in 1978 in the Archdiocese of Newark as the first Catholic organization to develop a diocesan-wide, parish spiritual renewal and evangelization process. The process, named RENEW, was aimed at revitalizing parish life in light of the mandates of Vatican II.

Word of RENEW soon spread and other dioceses in the United States and Canada began to implement it. Dioceses around the world followed; they imported and inculturated it. To date, the RENEW process in its varied forms has touched the lives of over 25 million individuals in church communities and campus communities across six continents. This includes over 150 United States dioceses and another 130 worldwide.

This Spirit-filled effort has been possible because in the thirty years since RENEW International began, as our Church and our world faced an array of pastoral needs, we have sought to respond by offering innovative, theologically sound, and pastorally appropriate processes and resources.

Sowing Seeds has come from fertile ground. Our hope is that *Sowing Seeds* will serve small community leaders/ facilitators well, whether they participate in one of our RENEW processes such as *Why Catholic?/¿Por qué ser católico?, Healing the Body of Christ/Sanando el Cuerpo de Cristo, ARISE Together in Christ*, RENEW Africa, RENEW Theology on Tap, or Campus RENEW or another process, or simply serve as leader/facilitator of a small community. It is for all those who are looking for a wealth of practical and inspirational material to enhance the ministry of being a small community leader/facilitator. In the words of RENEW International's Mission Statement, *Sowing Seeds* is for those who want to

> "foster spiritual renewal in the Catholic tradition
> by empowering individuals and communities
> to encounter God in everyday life,
> deepen and share faith,
> and connect faith with action."

A LETTER TO SMALL COMMUNITY LEADERS

Any time and forever in the Year of our Lord

Dear Small Community Leader,

Thank you for saying yes to being a leader of a small group or a small Christian community. This is a special ministry you have agreed to and we pray it will be a blessed time for you and for the members of your small community.

In small communities people grow into a greater awareness of the revelation of God. When Jesus began his public life, he gathered disciples around him and planted seeds of faith, hope, and love. He shared who he was, what he believed, what his values were, and his love of God, whom he called "Abba" or Father. His disciples observed that if someone was in need, he showed compassion; if someone was sick, he often healed that person; if someone was being treated unjustly, Jesus would confront the injustice or address the situation. By his actions, they learned more about him and what he stood for. Sometimes they saw that

> I planted,
> Apollos watered,
> but God gave the growth.
>
> 1 CORINTHIANS 3:6

he sought out a quiet or desert place to pray to his Abba. Through his words and actions, he revealed to them his relationship with his Abba.

Christians come to know God or Abba through knowing Jesus Christ. As Catholic Christians, we gather as disciples in Jesus' name in the larger community we call Church to celebrate Eucharist and the other sacraments. In small communities we come as Christians to pray; to explore what the Scriptures mean to us, especially through the teachings of the Church; to develop a more personal relationship with God; to experience community; and to examine how we can best live out the Word of God in our daily lives. Gradually, we share who we are, what we believe, and what our relationship with God is. As we share the Word of God and listen to others share faith, we relate Scripture and others' reflections on Scripture to our own lives. In other words, we make connections that give greater meaning to our faith lives. We come to know Jesus in a dynamic, life-giving way. We deepen our own faith and grow together in community.

In small Christian communities we also hear the Spirit's invitation for a more complete response to God's love and because we have the support of others in our own small community, we often have the courage and ability to profoundly affect society through our response.

All this is possible because the Spirit of God has led you and others like you to this moment and to this ministry of being a small community leader. You will be sowers of the Word of God. Trust the Spirit of God working in you and in the lives of each member of your small Christian community. Celebrate your faith with others and enjoy your ministry. Others will catch your spirit and enjoy the experience too. Henry David Thoreau once said, "Though I do not believe that a plant will spring up where no seed has been, I have great faith in a seed. Convince me that you have a seed there, and I am prepared to expect wonders." Who knows what wonders God has in store for you and your small Christian community?

Perhaps there may be times when you ask yourself, Why did I ever say yes? Then consider the opposite question, What if I didn't say yes? You would have missed the opportunity of a lifetime to be an instrument of grace for others. You will never know how many people's lives have been touched by your saying yes. The ripple effect might astound you.

What bonds of friendship did you form? In how many ways did you grow because you said yes? What new ideas did you learn about that will help you in the future? How many more people are now praying for you than might have if you didn't say yes? Your yes continues to bear fruit now and well into the future.

With our prayers and loving support,
The RENEW International Team

SAMPLE SCHEDULES
FOR SMALL COMMUNITIES

Whenever small communities gather together, it is wise to have a schedule to follow. On the next page are two schedules:

- the first for either an hour (with only one reflection and sharing) or an hour and a half (with two moments of reflection and sharing);
- the second, for two hours.

The one-hour schedule is what we would suggest for college-based faith-sharing groups.

At the very first gathering, members of a small community need to agree to the length of time they will spend together each session. The small community leader follows the schedule, yet needs to be flexible enough to adjust to the needs of the group and/or to allow for the stirrings of the Holy Spirit in the community.

Becoming accustomed to a simple routine such as this frees everyone from always having to figure out what comes next. It allows all to simply sink into the deeper parts of themselves and listen attentively to God.

The small community may decide to stay after the meeting for a short informal social gathering. Usually this gathering is no more than fifteen minutes or a half hour.

1 HOUR OR 1½ HOUR SCHEDULE

The one-hour schedule omits steps 5 and 6.

Introductions *(when the group is new or when someone joins the group)*

1. Opening Prayer	5 minutes
2. Sharing Action Response*	10 minutes
3. Reflection	10 minutes
4. Sharing Questions	15 minutes
[5. Reflection	10 minutes
6. Sharing Questions	20 minutes]
7. Action Response	15 minutes
8. Closing Prayer/Looking Ahead	5 minutes

In Session 1, during the time for Sharing Action Response, briefly introduce yourself. You will begin Sharing Action Response during Session 2.

2 HOUR SCHEDULE

Introductions *(when the group is new or when someone joins the group)*

1. Sharing Action Response*	20 minutes
2. Opening Prayer	15 minutes
3. Reflection	15 minutes
4. Sharing Questions	30 minutes
5. Action Response	15 minutes
6. Closing Prayer/Looking Ahead	10 minutes
7. Informal Gathering	15 minutes

In Session 1, during the time for Sharing Action Response, briefly introduce yourself. You will begin Sharing Action Response during Session 2.

FAQS OF SMALL COMMUNITY LEADERS

What is a small Christian community?

A Christian community is a group of people who are bonded by and strive to live by Jesus' vision and values. A small Christian community or a small church community is a group of people who come together in an ongoing way within the Christian tradition to pray, to reflect on a passage of Scripture, to share their life stories in light of the Word, and then to commit to live out the Word in their daily lives. Another way of saying this might be: a group of people committed to one another, to God, and to the world who desire the gospel to touch every aspect of their lives.

What happens in a small Christian community (SCC)?

As people reflect on a passage from Scripture they pray about how that passage relates to their lives. In sharing that experience with others in a small community,

> **Before the seed there comes the thought of bloom.**
>
> E. B. WHITE

they are sharing faith. In telling their story, they often come to new realizations of where God has been in their lives or what God may be saying to them now. As people listen to others share faith they often realize that God has been working similarly in their own lives. Usually those in small communities develop an appreciation of each other and also a deeper understanding of how God moves in peoples' lives. Participants may form relationships that have a profound and lasting influence in their lives. They offer loving support to each other, and try to connect their faith to their everyday life situations.

How often does a SCC meet?

Participants usually agree to meet on a regular basis, whether that is weekly, bi-weekly, or monthly. When a community is involved in a particular program, they often make a commitment for a segment of the program, for example, six weeks, or for the entire length of the program.

What is faith sharing?

Faith sharing refers to the shared reflections on the action of God in one's life experience as related to Scripture and the faith of the Church. Faith sharing is not primarily factual learning. In that sense, it is different from discussion, problem solving, or Scripture study. The purpose of faith sharing is to facilitate an encounter between a person in the concrete circumstances of his/her life and a loving God, leading to a conversion of heart. Faith sharing requires a person to tap into his/her own life experiences, to internalize them and connect them with the experience of God in their lives.

Should each person have his/her own Bible?

The leader may encourage each person who does not own a Bible to purchase one. All ought to use the Bible to read and reflect on the Scripture passage in the upcoming session. It is helpful for members to bring their Bibles to each session in case they are invited to read, or if someone makes reference to a particular passage during the session, all may want to read it in their own Bibles. However, when one person proclaims the reading at the session, it is much more effective for all members to listen to the proclamation rather than read along. In this way, all can be open to the Word touching their hearts.

Why become a small community leader?

Being a small community leader is a graced ministry. By being a small community leader a person often recognizes more clearly how God is acting in his/her life. Consequently, by facilitating this process the leader helps others to recognize and take ownership of how God is acting in their lives.

What is the role of a small community leader?

The role of a small community leader is twofold:

1. to create a welcoming atmosphere that gives participants the freedom and encouragement to share faith, one whereby the participants will know that the leader is a facilitator and not a teacher;

2. to keep the meeting on track, not letting it wander into other agendas.

What is the best way to prepare for the meeting?

One of the best ways to prepare is to meet each participant beforehand, giving him/her the materials to be used during the meeting and inviting each to prepare for the first session. As soon as the leader receives the list of those in the group, she/he may begin to pray daily for each person. Telling participants they are being prayed for at the first meeting will truly help them to feel special. The leader also needs to pray and reflect on the materials beforehand, so he/she can be at ease, not thinking about what next to say and focus greater attention on the participants.

In addition, by preparing a warm and friendly environment for the gathering participants will feel welcome. Roles may be shared. Someone may be invited to lead the prayer. Music is usually suggested. However, if the music is unavailable or not known, other selections may be chosen. Ensuring that the CD/cassette player works or that a musician will accompany the singing will help the meeting to go smoothly. Readers of Scripture may be chosen before the meeting so they are prepared to proclaim the Word of God. Participants may take turns providing refreshments for a brief social at the end of the meeting.

What is the best way to create a climate where all are welcome?

For the first meeting, the leader welcomes each individual as he/she arrives, helps make introductions, and when the whole group is assembled, welcomes the entire group and makes sure everyone knows everyone else. A simple icebreaker can help to do this. During this first meeting, it would be wise for the leader to help the group agree to certain ground rules that will help ensure a smooth process for the meeting (see A Sample Small Community Commitment, page 49).

In subsequent meetings, the leader greets each person, introduces any newcomers to the group, and occasionally checks in with the members to see how they are enjoying the group. During the faith-sharing process, the leader needs to be very attentive to respect each person in the small community, encouraging each person to share on the level where he/she feels comfortable. The honesty and openness of the leader will assist the community's growth.

How can a leader establish a sense of trust in the community?

At the very first meeting of the small community, the leader needs to speak about the importance of confidentiality, and a commitment to an atmosphere of confidentiality needs to be agreed upon by the whole group. Once this is done, a climate of trust grows. Often someone will share a life experience that is very meaningful for the group to hear, yet it is also very personal. That person expects everyone in the group to hold that experience in confidence. Confidentiality means that what is shared in the group is held in sacred trust. Participants may not share the information with anyone else unless permission is asked of the one who shared. Confidentiality permits each person to share honestly. Confidentiality is inherent in the very essence of small Christian communities.

How does the leader ensure a smooth meeting?

The leader wants to establish an easy flow to the meeting, not rushing the content. He/she needs to begin and end on time, keeping to the timeframe all have agreed upon. (The leader may have a small clock in the room and occasionally glance at it to keep the process moving or may appoint a timekeeper to gently remind the leader when there are twenty minutes left.) Very importantly, the leader wants to be sure to leave sufficient time for the action response section (15 minutes).

Should the leader speak first in the small community to get things rolling?

The leader ought to try not to speak first, but hold his/her contribution until a few have spoken. If the leader answers first, he/she may create a teacher role or be seen as the teacher. The leader is not meant to be a teacher. The leader is there to assure a smooth transition through the process of faith sharing as outlined in the materials.

What should I do if one person dominates the conversation?

Encourage participants to wait to share a second time until others who wish to do so have spoken. If someone continues to dominate, speak to that person privately after the meeting and respectfully ask him/her to allow others to have their time to share.

What if there is a period of silence during our small community gathering?

Silence is a vital part of the overall faith-sharing process. It is important that the leader be willing to wait for others to speak and learn to be comfortable with silence. Participants are given a moment of silence to reflect before any sharing begins. A period of silence might occur between individual sharings. That allows people time to think about what they are going to say. God often speaks to us in the silence.

What should I do if a faith-sharing question is difficult or if most people don't understand the questions?

Try to reword the question. See if people nod in agreement that they understand the rephrased question. Or tell them how you interpreted that question when you prepared beforehand.

How would you handle a participant who is reluctant to speak?

The leader might remind participants that the entire community is responsible for participating and faith sharing. Certainly the leader can share his/her thoughts, which in turn may encourage others to share. If a person never shares the leader may, after three or so meetings, speak to the person privately to see if they are comfortable with the process. However, if a person wants to be in a group and not share aloud she/he should also be welcome. A poignant story has been told about a person who was reluctant to speak:

A woman in a small community never joined in the conversation for about a year. When she finally did speak, she thanked the other members for letting her be herself in the group and then revealed that when she entered the group she had just been released from a mental health facility. She told the members how they had helped to heal her just by letting her be there. The others in the group were very happy for her that she was finally able to share her story.

This true story illustrates the respect that needs to be given to each individual member and the immense power of mutual support in a small Christian community.

How can a leader encourage the spiritual growth of the community and its individual members?

A leader promotes the spiritual growth of the community and its individual members by creating a prayerful atmosphere at meetings, by encouraging participation and the sharing of our Christian faith at the meetings, and by encouraging participants to spend quality time each day in personal prayer and reflection on the Scriptures, and when possible, by participating frequently in the Eucharist.

How does a leader move the community to action?

By using the small Christian community materials well, the leader will allow time for the action response section of the session. People want to make a difference in their lives and in the world around them. They are usually not satisfied to remain centered on themselves. Leaders can always urge the small community to consider how what they shared can be brought to life situations, to the needs of their parish, city or town, or to the world around them. Action flowing out of the small community gathering is essential for the growth of individuals and the community (see also chapter entitled, "Leaven for Transforming the World," pages 19-25).

What if someone raises a theological question?

Small community leaders should not feel they have to worry about answering theological questions. The nature of the meeting is faith sharing. If a theological or scriptural question arises, the leader may say she/he will try to find the answer, ask someone else to research the answer, or seek guidance from the pastor or staff and report back to the group the following week. If it seems feasible, the leader may invite the pastor or a staff member to come to the group to discuss the question or topic.

What if a priest, religious sister or brother, deacon, or staff person joins our small community?

If any of the above persons joins the small community, they join to participate in the same way everyone else does. The leader needs to be careful not to defer his/her role to another.

What if someone shares some very personal situation and seeks counsel from the group?

Small communities are not intended for counseling or problem solving. Small community gatherings are an inappropriate setting to deal with emotionally-laden issues of a personal nature. The leader should simply bring the community back to prayer or faith sharing (see the AARR Method, on pages 11-12). The leader is clearly not to enter the realm of attempting to treat people with emotional feelings such as depression, anxiety, or intense anger. Should another member of the group move in this direction, beyond faith sharing, the leader should again bring the community back to faith sharing. Afterwards, perhaps during the social, the leader might speak with the person and suggest the person seek the assistance of a pastoral counselor. The facilitator may say something like, "Thank you for trusting us. Did you ever think of sharing your anxiety (depression or intense anger) with a pastoral counselor?"

CHARACTERISTICS OF AUTHENTIC SMALL CHRISTIAN COMMUNITIES

In their Pastoral Statement, *Called and Gifted for the Third Millennium*, the United States Catholic Bishops speak of the value of small Christian communities. They state that "Small church communities not only foster the faith of individuals; they are living cells that build up the Body of Christ. They are to be signs and instruments of unity. As basic units of the parish, they serve to increase the corporate life and mission of the parish by sharing in its life generously with their talents and support."

They also set out specific characteristics of authentic small Christian communities:

▶ obedience to the word of God

▶ common prayer

From the communion that Christians experience in Christ there immediately flows the communion which they experience with one another: all are branches of a single vine, namely, Christ.

CHRISTIFIDELES LAICI, 18

▶ a commitment of time to one another for building personal relationships

▶ meaningful participation in the life of their local parish

▶ some form of apostolic mission to the wider society

▶ an adherence to the Catholic faith

▶ an explicit relationship of communion with the Church

Small community leaders can take a leadership role in their parishes by working with their pastors to ensure that these characteristics are incorporated into the life of the small communities. In doing this they bring their wisdom and expertise from their family life and their work situations, which greatly enhances the quality of the small communities. When small community members take ownership of these characteristics and they are clearly evident to the parish and wider community, the parish will be aglow with vibrantly authentic small Christian communities.

AARR FACILITATION METHOD

Overcoming Issues, Complaints, Tangents in Faith Sharing

When a person strays from the process or says something inappropriate during the small community meeting, the leader can apply the AARR Method to get the group back on track. This simple method presents a win/win situation for all: the individual, the group, and the leader. It involves active listening, respecting the person who raised the question or issue, and refocusing. This simple method has four components:

1. **A**cknowledge what is said
2. **A**ffirm the person
3. **R**edirect the conversation
4. **R**efocus the question

A person who sows seeds of kindness enjoys a perpetual harvest.

ANONYMOUS

ACKNOWLEDGE   *Demonstrate that you've heard the person*

"You certainly feel strongly about this."
"I can see you've done a lot of thinking on this subject."
"It must have taken some courage to share that with us."
"You sound very frustrated."

AFFIRM   *Validate the person for who he or she is*

"You really seem interested in this."
"I can see why you feel that way."
"That's something we've all thought about."
"Our hearts go out to you and we will pray for you."

REDIRECT   *Show how the issue/complaint cannot and should not be addressed in the faith-sharing session*

"At this session we are not going to be able to change the Church's/media's/society's position."
"We're not trained counselors/theologians/teachers, etc."
"After the faith sharing, as our mission activity, perhaps we can write letters to the editor."

REFOCUS   *Get the group back to faith sharing*

"Even though we can't resolve (the issue/complaint), we can grow in our faith by looking at the material before us."
"I'm glad you mentioned that ... it brings us back to the subject we began with ...."
"What we can do is get back to listening to how Christ is working in our lives."

FIVE ELEMENTS OF SMALL CHRISTIAN COMMUNITIES

As a small Christian community leader, you are empowering individuals and the small community as a whole to encounter God, to deepen and share their faith, and to connect this faith with their everyday lives through their action responses. The five essential elements of prayer, faith sharing, mutual support, learning, and action are the tools to make this happen. Each one is necessary to the life of a small Christian community. As a small Christian community leader, then, you hold the responsibility to ensure these elements are part of the life of the small Christian community.

While one or more of these elements may be more prominent or take more time during the meeting, the remainder may be more evident in the ongoing life of the small community members, for the life of a small Christian community naturally extends beyond the meeting. Therefore, these five elements become a way of life for the

> **Think small. Planting tiny seeds in the small space given you can change the whole world or, at the very least, your view of it.**
>
> Linus Mundy

small community members, a spiritual path. Each, in turn, will be briefly explained here. (For a more extended discussion on these elements, see *Small Christian Communities: A Vision of Hope, Revised and Expanded*, by Thomas A. Kleissler, Margo A. LeBert, and Mary C. McGuinness, Paulist Press, 2003.)

PRAYER

Prayer is the foundation of our Christian life and for that reason we both begin and end our small Christian community gatherings with set times for prayer. Prayer takes many forms—silent, vocal, private, communal, meditative, contemplative—and small community leaders have the opportunity to use these various forms during their small Christian community meetings. Just as the leader is encouraged to prayerfully prepare before the meeting, so too, the leader is urged to encourage the small community members to pray in preparation. The more we pray, the more prayer becomes second nature to us, wherever we are—while walking, riding a bus or train, or driving a car. Others in the small community may have a favorite way of praying and can share or take a turn in leading the community in prayer.

When we come together as members of a small community, we gather for community prayer or shared prayer. We recognize the shared faith experience that brings us together. Jesus tells us "where two or three are gathered in my name, I am there among them (Matthew 18:20). Community prayer, then, can be a powerful experience of the presence of God in our midst. It enriches and strengthens the faith we share and deepens our relationships with one another and with God. Community prayer can be silent or vocal. It takes many forms: in a small community, the predominant form of community prayer is faith sharing, but as we together sing, listen to or read Scripture, reflect silently, pray for ourselves and others, we are also engaged in communal prayer.

Some members of the group may have difficulty sharing faith during the meeting, but when they pray aloud communally, particularly during prayers of petition, they are sharing faith. Through their prayer they are implying that they trust the group and that God hears their call. It may take time, but this is the first step for many members to sharing faith. They may first begin by saying, "I want to pray for my sister, _____, who is suffering from _____." Eventually, these believers share what's in their heart. (For more on prayer, see section entitled "Resources.")

FAITH SHARING

The heart of small Christian community meetings is faith sharing. Faith sharing is sharing some facet of one's relationship with God or connecting a personal event with a passage of Scripture or an aspect of our Christian faith. Listening to another share faith gives a glimpse of someone else's relationship with God or how they see God moving in their lives. Ultimately, it gives us glimpses of how God is working in our lives and in the world. As Henri Nouwen has said, "My deepest vocation is to be a witness to the glimpses of God I am allowed to see."

At a small church community meeting, a passage from sacred Scripture is read. Members listen attentively to hear what God is saying at this moment in their lives. Often they may be asked to say a word or a phrase that struck them or a feeling the passage evoked in them. This is a simple form of sharing faith. As they read the reflection for the particular session, they hear again the wisdom of others and relate it to their lives. Faith-sharing questions follow the reflections. Small Christian community leaders need to be particularly careful to allow a short period of silence to allow members to reflect on what they have heard and to read over the faith-sharing questions before the faith sharing begins.

As participants share their faith, others need to listen. No response is necessary except, perhaps, for the facilitator to quietly say thank you to the person who has shared. All should be given the opportunity to share once before someone shares a second time. Leaders need to encourage all to share, but to be respectful of those who wish to remain silent.

For small Christian communities to be worthy of their name, carrying out the mission Christ gave to his Church must always be the primary focus. Faith sharing that focuses on the self-interest of the group will, in time, have the effect of atrophy on the group. The Holy Spirit is a fire vigorously moving a healthy community to a ministry of loving service.

MUTUAL SUPPORT

As small community members share and get to know one another, relationships naturally form and people begin to support one another in prayer as well as in other ways. If someone mentions a sick or injured family member or friend, or if someone loses a loved one, members may reach out by bringing meals or offering other services. As members pray, they mention their needs and later during the social time, members have the opportunity to ask about the particular person or situation and offer their support. Often when a crisis occurs in a person's life, the seeds of faith are challenged and that person can be more open to God working in and through their lives. As small community members support one another in crisis, suffering, joy, or celebration, spiritual friendships form—often lasting a lifetime, sometimes beyond the life of a small community.

LEARNING

When small community members gather and share, they naturally learn from one another. They learn how others experience God in their lives; they learn how different people pray and what they read to nourish their faith life; they learn how others respond to the Word of God through their actions; and much more. By using the Bible to prepare beforehand and while at the meeting, those who are new to small communities may be learning, perhaps for the first time, how to use the Bible and how to pray while using a passage from Scripture. Through giving simple directions and waiting patiently while a person finds a particular passage, a small community leader can begin to facilitate this type of learning.

In preparation for a small community meeting, the small community leader may ask the members to read and reflect on the Scripture passage beforehand. When doing this, encourage members to listen to what God is saying to them in their lives. This is a form of meditation, which requires attentiveness. The *Catechism of the Catholic Church* tells us that when we do this, we engage our "thought, imagination, emotion, and desire. We do this to deepen our convictions of faith, prompt the conversion of our heart, and strengthen our will to follow Christ" (2708).

In addition, the leader may encourage others to share what spiritual books they are reading or what their favorite spiritual books are. Occasionally, members may take the time to share in depth what a book or DVD/videotape has meant to them. Others may share about a retreat, a day of reflection, a workshop they participated in, and/or a conference they attended that nourished their spiritual growth.

ACTION

In his Letter, St. James reminds us to "be doers of the Word and not merely hearers who deceive themselves" (1:22). As a response to the Word of God and the shared word among the small community members, there is always an invitation to respond. Ideally the response ought to flow from the Word and the sharing. However, in the participants' faith-sharing resources there are usually suggested action responses, which may inspire or prompt participants to take a specific action. Most often and especially in the beginning, members decide on a personal action response. Later, they may decide to take on a communal action, which may be a one-time event such as participating in a town council meeting, or an ongoing action, such as cooking for a soup kitchen and volunteering to serve there once a month or weekly. As a small community leader, you can encourage members who seem reluctant to make a decision to act by asking themselves questions, such as the following:

- How shall I live out the Word of God this week? or

- What is the Spirit of God prompting me to do? or

▶ How is God inviting me to change my life this week?

It is wise for a small community leader to allow at least fifteen minutes for this part of the session. In addition the leader can provide a brief summary of what has been shared and ask participants to reflect on what God may be calling them to do or what they need to change in their lives.

RENEW International suggests three steps the small community leader may take to facilitate and strengthen participants' involvement with the action step:

1. Give participants enough time to decide what action response they will take.

2. Invite them to write down the action they plan to take and then name it aloud. By hearing what others have decided, reluctant members may be inspired to do the same or a similar action.

3. At the following small community meeting, allow time for participants to share briefly how they did with their action response. This may encourage others who would be hesitant to take a similar step. If someone forgot to do it, they would simply say they forgot. Hopefully, listening to others share their action may motivate them to follow through on future action response commitments.

Action does not necessarily mean adding on "something else." It means following God's call to live our faith. Sometimes God calls us to think differently, to pray, differently, to behave differently.

As a small group grows in living out the five essential elements of small Christian communities, it becomes a living witness to the Word of God. By God's grace as members incorporate these elements in their lives and, therefore, in the life of the community, they may truly come to be called a small Christian community.

LEAVEN FOR TRANSFORMING THE WORLD

Jesus invited disciples into community, where they could tell their stories within the larger context of his story. He formed them for mission and sent them out two-by-two. Their theology and practice was shaped and formed by action, experience, and reflection in their community. So too is ours. We need a small community to come back to, so we can reflect upon our experience with others.

In the formation of small communities we speak of the inner journey and the outer journey—really one journey. Our quest to know God more intimately should bring us into the depths of the interior life. On the other hand, a clearer understanding of the mission of Jesus and the movement of the Holy

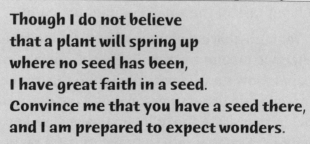

Though I do not believe
that a plant will spring up
where no seed has been,
I have great faith in a seed.
Convince me that you have a seed there,
and I am prepared to expect wonders.

HENRY DAVID THOREAU

Spirit in our hearts should propel us into exciting new levels of outreach and justice.

St. Edith Stein tells us, "The deeper one is drawn into God, the more one needs to go out of oneself—out into the world, that is, to carry the divine life into it."

Traditionally there have been three main classifications of outreach:

1. *Projects or direct service:* e.g., cooking for or working in a soup kitchen.

2. *Systemic change:* that is, change that affects all aspects or levels of an institution or society, e.g., giving people skills that will help them in the future, e.g., working as a Literacy Volunteer or helping with voter registration. Systemic change can be temporary or has the possibility of providing long lasting results.

3. *Advocacy:* speaking or writing on behalf of another's cause, e.g., writing to legislators or writing a letter to the editor of a local newspaper about a specific issue or visiting a school board member to speak about a particular issue you feel strongly about.

Small communities provide the climate for engaging participants in the process of reflection, a way to let the gospel touch every aspect of their lives. Helping small Christian communities to move beyond themselves to show the same type of love and fairness that Jesus showed or to be leaven for transforming the world seems to be the most difficult task of the small community leader.

Yet faith-sharing communities provide an ideal climate for reflecting on and responding to the social dimension of the gospel. How do we invite people to this process? How do we surface and address personal and civic responsibility and social issues? On the following pages are five strategies that enable the community to reflect on and respond to the social dimension of the gospel.

FIVE STRATEGIES

1. THE SOCIAL INQUIRY APPROACH OF OBSERVE, JUDGE, ACT

RENEW International proposes the social inquiry approach of Observe, Judge, Act as the best means of achieving action. The social inquiry approach is not one more faith-sharing exercise but a method for a faith-sharing group that is precisely designed to help people come to specific and outward-oriented action that will have social impact. It is a proven method for helping people to put their faith in action. (For additional information, see the chapter on Resources, pages 61-63.) People do not have to travel far to effect change. They can begin to bear a Christian influence where they already are in their own city or town.

There are three simple steps and when used often they become a way of life:

OBSERVE   Be aware of the reality of the environment. This step, the Observe, is designed to uncover the facts about a particular situation or event rather than draw from personal opinions.

JUDGE   Apply the mind and heart of Jesus. What would Jesus do? To judge a Christian approach, look to Scripture, the teachings of the Church, and the wisdom of the Holy Spirit working in your small community.

ACT   Take concrete action. Actions must be very specific and concrete as to who, when, how, and where. Actions may be individual and/or communal. They may be very small, but must be doable, e.g., writing a letter to a legislator, visiting new neighbors to welcome them to the neighborhood or apartment building. A realtor came to the simple, yet significant, action of putting voter registration forms in packets for new and prospective home owners. Later she was instrumental in involving all the realtors in her company in building homes for Habitat for Humanity.

These small actions help people come to deeper awareness and greater and more significant actions. A positive experience with small actions will usually encourage small community members to grow in confidence to attempt more complex and/or significant actions. Members need to have the freedom to progress at their own rate.

2. LISTEN TO PROPHETIC PEOPLE IN SMALL CHRISTIAN COMMUNITIES

A prophet is one who speaks for God. When in your life have you been in the presence of a prophet, a person who challenged you to live a better life? Sometimes we may be startled by what someone is saying, but good listening requires we be open to the possibility of seeds of wisdom coming from all group members. One person can make a difference.

In small Christian communities, there may be a person or persons who call others to a particular stance or situation. For example, a member of a small community may have visited people held in an immigration detention center. As the person shares the experience of their visits back in the small community, other members may realize that those held in detention are their brothers and sisters and be inspired to join him or her in visiting others who are held. Again, someone may see the need for affordable housing in the local area and challenge the small community to action to advocate for it at a town council meeting.

It is always good to recognize and thank a person who has been a prophet or who has challenged us to follow a specific call. A priest received a letter from a friend who was on retreat. One question the friend was reflecting on was this: At what time in your life have you received a prophet who challenged you? The friend's response was contained in his letter:

> "Yes! There were several. You were one and you taught and inspired and stretched and challenged me. To this day your life is a light for me and thousands. Just a note to let you know and to thank you warmly."

At what time in your life have you received a prophet who challenged you? How have you been a prophet to challenge others?

3. KNOW OR BE WITH SOMEONE WHO IS POOR

When asked what we as North Americans can do about poverty, a prophet might very well respond, "Get to know one person who is poor." Knowing just one person, a family, or a group of people who are poor or who have been treated unfairly will expand our horizons, widen our perceptions, and hopefully move us to pray for them and ultimately do whatever we are inspired to do to help them.

Today it is becoming increasingly popular for students on campus to have an immersion experience (e.g., in Appalachia); or for families to do volunteer work or to take a working vacation in different countries or even in the United States in those areas devastated by hurricanes (e.g., New Orleans). Parents, children, and teens alike are involved for a week or more. They may begin to learn a new language and are exposed to a different culture. All the while they may be helping a family, village, or town, for example, to plant trees, dig wells, build or repair homes, or be involved in sustainable development.

Having an immersion experience of being with the poor or getting to know someone from a third world country can be a very meaningful experience. Volunteer opportunities are intended to benefit the recipients of the aid, but they also deliver many positive side effects for the volunteers themselves. To learn from each other, to form true friendships with others, to pray for that person or persons by name, to correspond, and, perhaps, to visit again are true gifts for both volunteers and recipients. Volunteers will have a better understanding of how to address serious social issues at home and abroad. They will also have made a difference in making our world a better place, one of the basic heart wishes of most people.

4. EMPOWERMENT PAIRS

The following exercise is a very simple method of helping people uncover their skills or gifts, so they can use them in different settings to help bring about a more fair and loving society.

Step 1.   Choose a partner. Decide who will go first/second.

Step 2. (4 minutes) First person—Think of a time when you were dissatisfied with something in your life, and you decided to make a change and were successful (for example: stopped biting your nails, got stop sign put into neighborhood, etc.). Now think of what skills, personal traits, or talents it took for you to make this change (for example: patience, etc.). Tell your partner about it.

Step 3. (3 minutes) Now put your heads together and think about how you could use these same skills and personal traits as you work for a more loving and fair world.

Step 4. (5 minutes) Switch. The second person now tells their success story in the same way. (A facilitator can say when five minutes are up.)

Step 5. (3 minutes) Then work together to see how the same skills and traits could be used in working for a more loving and fair world.

Step 6.   Large Group Sharing—Partners share each other's success stories.

Step 7.   Commitment Step—Each person says aloud how she/he would like to use his/her skills in a new way for the betterment of the world, that is, what action step each will take.

Adapted from Despair and Personal Power in the Nuclear Age *by Joanna Macy and a process used at the Cuernavaca Center for Intercultural Dialogue and Development*

5. REFLECTION QUESTIONS FOR A GATHERING OF SMALL COMMUNITY LEADERS

It is extremely helpful for small community leaders to gather together occasionally to pray, to support one another, and to share insights on their ministry. Below are three questions that may assist them to motivate small communities to further the mission of Jesus:

❯ Honestly evaluate how many small church groups in the larger community (parish, chaplaincy, campus) are engaged in significant action, especially social action.

❯ What inhibits people from extending beyond their personal and communal comfort zone?

❯ How can we motivate our small communities to conscientiously be about action, that is, to fully engage in the mission of Jesus? What steps will you take in this regard?

PROJECT PLANNING

Many times individual members of the small Christian community choose specific acts as a response to the Scripture, reflection, and faith sharing. Sometimes the community as a whole takes on a particular action. In this section, we speak of the latter.

All small groups, at some time, are involved in some specific planning, perhaps, for a particular activity, program, or project. While most people have some experience in planning events and projects (within their family or work situations), it is helpful to have a clear idea of the points that should be included as they plan. If we use the example of a small group deciding to undertake a project, we can consider these questions:

Why?

Are all members of the community clear on why the community has decided to do the project and how this project fits in with the life and purpose of the community?

Who?

Who is doing the project and for whom is the project being

Don't judge each day by the harvest you reap, but by the seeds you plant.
Robert Louis Stevenson

done or to whom is it directed? It is important that the community be very clear on which members have specific responsibilities in the project. It is helpful to keep a written record of these responsibilities.

What?

Is everyone clear on the exact nature and content of the project?

Where?

What are the location and environment of the project?

When?

What is the schedule for the project? It is often helpful to develop a timeline which shows what tasks related to the project have to be done and when each task will be completed.

How?

The "how" question is answered by an overview of the project which includes steps to be taken, tasks to be done, persons responsible for the tasks, and the resources needed to accomplish the tasks.

How evaluated?

The group should determine how and when the project will be evaluated. Questions for evaluation would include: Did the project achieve its goals? Was the group faithful to tasks and timeline?

When the entire community takes on a project, the leader has to be aware of the task each member of the community has agreed to do, be in touch with each member to see how they are progressing, and offer encouragement. When someone is responsible for overseeing the project, it is far more likely to be completed.

TIPS FOR
SMALL COMMUNITY
LEADERS

A good small community leader is warm, open, friendly, and sensitive. The leader attempts to create a climate of understanding and acceptance while avoiding inclinations to control. The leader is not the "expert," but rather a community member who facilitates the small community, freely acknowledges personal limitations, and welcomes new information, ideas, and insights.

What follows are some concrete suggestions for small community leaders who facilitate faith-sharing small groups. These suggestions are grouped into four categories: sensitivity to people, spirituality, broad vision, and a sense of celebration. The leaders themselves are not expected to undertake all the tasks listed; however, they need to have a working knowledge of them and be able to elicit others' help in ensuring they are carried out.

> Unless a grain of wheat
> falls into the earth and dies,
> it remains just a single grain;
> but if it dies, it bears much fruit.
>
> JOHN 12:24

SENSITIVITY TO PEOPLE

A good small community leader knows the importance of the virtue of hospitality and implements or invites the person providing the venue and hospitality to implement the following:

- ▶ the physical arrangement of the room: individuals should be able to see and hear one another clearly. Having chairs in a circle helps communication and lessens a common misconception that the sharing is a "class."

- ▶ the setting of the environment: having the Bible displayed, using candles (and other symbols), music, pictures (newspaper articles and/or headlines, photos), etc., can do much to create a prayerful, reflective atmosphere. This calls for planning.

- ▶ provision of refreshments: a common understanding that refreshments are ordinarily to be simple is important and avoids the danger of members trying to outdo one another. (It helps if different members bring the refreshments each week.) Serving refreshments during the meeting can be distracting. Determine with the group what custom they wish to adopt with regard to enjoying refreshments.

- ▶ limiting distractions: turn off televisions, computers, and cell phones; put purses, briefcases, and backpacks away.

- ▶ providing a sense of welcome, especially to new members: for example, introducing them to everyone.

- ▶ following up on absent members with a phone call or an email to let them know they were missed: checking on difficulties such as transportation (providing a ride if necessary).

A good small group cares about people and shows it in a variety of ways:

- ▶ admitting limitations. The leader can encourage honesty and openness in the group by his or her own willingness to acknowledge personal strengths and failures.

▶ encouraging those who may be shy or unsure of themselves. Speak to the individual over refreshments, ask for his or her reactions, affirm these and encourage sharing.

▶ motivating members to use their gifts and talents, and supporting members who minister to others in and beyond the group.

▶ being aware of joys, sorrows, and problems in the lives of individual members and their families and encouraging the group to be supportive. Sometimes, the birth of a child, sickness, and death in the family are events in which the group can share, offering loving, practical help. Some such situations may call for a special sensitivity. For example, a member who has lost his or her job may be embarrassed and suffering a lessening of self-esteem. In such a case, the leader could speak to the individual privately, offering support and also encouraging the member to trust enough to share the problem with the group. Others may be aware of suitable employment opportunities.

▶ being willing to share one's own struggles with the group. Part of caring for others is allowing them to care for us.

▶ challenging the group to greater honesty, authenticity, and commitment. The more honest and authentic the leader is, the more participants will feel comfortable in being their true selves. As the leader reveals his/her commitment to the small community and the action response that flows from the sharing, others will be inspired to do the same.

▶ encouraging the group to avoid **Red Flag Words**:

  • **generalizations:** people, everyone, you, they, no one, always, never, the Church, the parish, those people, the others ...

  • **judgmental words:** should, ought, cannot, fault, blame ...

  • **confrontational phrases:** you are ... why do/don't you ... how can/could you ... how come you ...

SPIRITUALITY

A good small community leader nurtures the spiritual growth of the community. The following are some practical ways of doing this:

▶ engage in prayer, reflection, spiritual reading.

▶ pray regularly for the group and each of its members.

▶ introduce different prayer forms such as centering prayer, meditation, praying with psalms. Mention the value of spiritual direction.

▶ suggest evenings or days of retreat and spiritual reading material. The parish staff can be an excellent resource in these areas.

▶ encourage individual members or the group to participate in the sacramental life, especially the Eucharist, as an expression of Christian spirituality and as fundamental to being Church.

▶ encourage all members to take responsibility for spiritual growth, to share resources with one another, and to challenge the group to a deeper spiritual life.

BROADER VISION

The continued life, authenticity, and vitality of the community require that the group look beyond itself. The leader can facilitate this outward vision in the following ways:

▶ call attention to the activities of the parish, the diocese, and the universal Church.

▶ stress the need for outreach and service within the community and in the wider civic and social arena.

▶ include a wide variety of concerns in the prayer, reflection, and ongoing learning of the community.

▶ encourage the group to see the connections between their own personal growth, development, and integrity and that of the community, Church, society, and the whole of creation.

▶ challenge the group to become more aware of the social teaching of the Church and specific social concerns through discussion, reading, and educational opportunities.*

SENSE OF CELEBRATION

A community also bonds if the members share socially. The leader could encourage opportunites such as the following:

▶ holiday celebrations (for example, caroling at Christmas time), which could include family members.

▶ involvement of members' families in special activities, for example, outreach actions, special prayer experiences, picnics, and camping weekends.

▶ celebrations of members' birthdays and special events in their lives.

---

* Catholic social teaching is the collection of social principles and moral teaching that addresses the economic, political, and social order. It is rooted in Scripture and Tradition. Catholic social teaching is expressed in a variety of official documents of the Church from the late nineteenth century to the present day (encyclicals, Council or Synod documents, pastoral letters). The cornerstone of this teaching is the value and dignity of each human being, as created in the image and likeness of God.

BUILDING COMMUNITY THROUGH LISTENING

Developing relationships and building community require that people really listen to one another. Listening helps both the speaker and the hearer to grow as persons. Good listening within a group increases the trust, openness, and understanding that make for authentic community. People who truly listen to one another are drawn together in a special bond.

Effective listening conveys acceptance, caring, and respect. The person who is listened to (the speaker) grows in a sense of self-worth. Good listening encourages sincerity and honesty. Often this helps the speaker come to a greater self-understanding.

At the same time, the listener feels valued and appreciated. Good listening requires that the listener enter into the thinking and experience of the other person and thus helps the listener to broaden perceptions and outlooks. Good listening helps an individual and a group to grow spiritually.

> **Flowers and fruit are only the beginning. In the seed lie the life and the future.**
>
> MARION ZIMMER BRADLEY

FOUR QUALITIES OF A GOOD LISTENER

(Based on On Listening to Another *by Douglas Steere)*

VULNERABILITY

Good listeners are exposed to the discomfort of having preconceived ideas changed. They run the risk of sometimes being hurt by the honesty that good listening can evoke. They become more exposed to the pain, frustration, and complexity of the human condition. In a word, they experience human limitations and yet remain hopeful because they believe that Jesus Christ has shared in their humanity.

ACCEPTANCE

Good listeners take the speaker at face value. Really listening means that the listener cannot expect the speaker to fit into his or her expectations. The speaker is respected and valued for who he or she really is. Such caring and respect for another mirrors the love God has for each person.

EXPECTANCY

Good listeners hope that in communicating, both speaker and listener will arrive at greater truth and deeper awareness of the beauty in both speaker and hearer. There is a sense that through the honest speaking and listening both speaker and listener will be renewed. Such hope and expectancy are basic to Christian faith.

CONSTANCY

Good listeners will patiently persevere in listening even when it is difficult, taxing, and complicated. There is a certain faithfulness to the speaker that says, "I'm with you through the 'thick and thin' of this conversation." Such a fidelity is a reflection of God's faithfulness.

The four qualities of a good listener mentioned above help prepare a person for the skill of effective listening. For the person of faith, good listening is not only a discipline, but also a sign of the healing and enlivening presence of God's Spirit.

THE "HOW TOs" OF EFFECTIVE LISTENING

Effective listening is following what another is thinking and feeling. It is understanding the meaning of what another is saying from that person's perspective. The ability to listen well rarely comes naturally. It is a skill that must be learned. However, the formal and informal education of most people has emphasized the ability to speak well with very little attention given to the ability to listen well. If small Christian communities are to realize the fullness of their potential, it is important that their members work to develop their skills, not only in speaking honestly and clearly, but also in listening effectively.

Additional suggestions for developing the skill of effective listening continue in the following section and in the next two chapters.

SUGGESTIONS FOR DEVELOPING THE SKILL OF LISTENING

GIVE PEOPLE TIME

Do not interrupt people until they have had the opportunity to express a full thought. People speak at different paces. Adjust to their rhythm. Resist the temptation to finish their sentences for them.

WORK AT CONCENTRATION

Try to put yourself in the speaker's place in order to understand his or her frame of reference or point of view.

LISTEN FOR CONTENT AND FEELING

Listen not just to the words but to the whole person. Pay attention to facial expressions, gestures, position of the body, and tone and intensity of the voice.

SHOW YOUR INTEREST

Make eye contact with the speaker. Avoid distracting movements and gestures that may suggest a lack of interest, for example, restlessness, crossing your arms, glancing at your watch or a clock. A relaxed manner will encourage the speaker.

ACTIVE LISTENING

Active listening is a technique to recognize and affirm what the other person is saying, without offering your own input. To engage in active listening, you name the *feeling* that underlies someone's comments, as well as the reason that this feeling may be present. It can take the form of "I hear that you're feeling _____ because of _____." This technique enables you as the listener to confirm what you heard, and it also provides the speaker with an opportunity to expand upon his/her remarks, if appropriate.

ASK CLARIFYING QUESTIONS

Ask questions that help you and the speaker come to a greater understanding of the topic. For example: "Can you tell me more about that?" "This is what I hear you saying …. Do I have it straight?" "What was that like for you?"

DELAY JUDGING

Don't make judgments too quickly. Wait to hear the whole message. Premature judging can cut off the speaker's sharing before the whole picture emerges and thus diminish understanding.

Effective listening requires concentration and sensitivity. Willingness to expend the effort needed for this kind of listening will depend on whether the hearer understands a reason for listening. The listener can be influenced by whether he or she thinks the message is important to hear. Very often, listening is also related to whether the hearer respects the speaker. To listen well, a person must genuinely believe that the one speaking is worthwhile and has something valuable to say.

BRIDGES TO EFFECTIVE LISTENING

LISTEN   by using my whole body. Let my body language show that I am listening (open body stance, direct eye contact, lean forward slightly).

LISTEN   by being truly present to the speaker and giving undivided attention (not doing something else at the same time I am supposedly listening).

LISTEN   by acknowledging the speaker's feelings. ("I can hear that you have a lot of feelings around this topic," "You sound very sad.") Don't minimize, sermonize, or negate.

> **The field has eyes, the wood has ears;**
> **I will look, be silent, and listen.**
>
> HIERONYMUS BOSCH

LISTEN   by observing. The words the speaker says are only part of the story. Be mindful of the facial expressions, tone of voice, and body language in order to better interpret what you are hearing. Do the words match the body language? If not, some clarifying is in order.

LISTEN   by putting aside my own needs. I need to allow the person to speak and not protect my comfort by changing the subject or making a joke to relieve tension. I can acknowledge that I may not have had a similar experience and so cannot know really how the speaker feels, but show nevertheless I do want to listen.

LISTEN   by keeping focused on the speaker and the speaker's experience, without planning my response or anticipating what the speaker will say before it is said.

LISTEN   by not problem solving, giving unasked for and unwanted advice, and remembering that the focus is to listen and not to "fix it."

LISTEN   by allowing the speaker's point of view, by giving up my need to be right, and by not arguing my own point.

LISTEN   by paraphrasing and asking clarifying questions so the speaker knows that I heard and understood what was said.

BARRIERS TO
EFFECTIVE LISTENING

MINIMIZING   downplaying someone's opinion:
"It could be worse" or "It will get better."

SERMONIZING   saying: "It's God's will." "You must have
faith."

SELECTING   choosing what is comfortable to listen to
or what fits your experience.

NEGATING   denying the other person his or her
feelings.
"You shouldn't feel that way."

PLANNING   thinking of a
response or
solution and not
really hearing.

ANTICIPATING   determining
what will be said
before it happens.

The seed never sees the flower.
ZEN SAYING

TOPPING   focusing on your own story:
                     "My story's better than your story."

ARGUING   debating to prove a point of view.

PACIFYING   agreeing in order to be liked or accepted:
                     "Of course," "I know what you mean,"
                     "How wonderful!" "Really?," "Uh huh …
                     uh huh," or "Great!"

REDIRECTING   changing the subject or "lightening up"
                     an uncomfortable atmosphere through
                     humor.

JUSTIFYING   maintaining a strong need to be right.

SHUTTING OUT   interrupting or cutting off another
                     person; paying no attention to the
                     previous comment.

NAMING YOUR SMALL CHRISTIAN COMMUNITY

Whether a small group has just begun to meet or a small Christian community has been meeting for some time, it may decide to choose a name for itself. Naming is a wonderful way to establish an identity for the group or to express the charism of the community. Some small communities may choose a patron saint—a saint who has special meaning for the group—or a particular title of the Blessed Virgin Mary if the group has special devotion to Mary. Another possibility might be choosing a term from a favorite Scripture passage from the Bible, for example, "The Sowers," "The Spirit of God Community," or "Salt of the Earth Community."

> I am the vine,
> you are the branches.
> Those who abide in me and I in them
> bear much fruit,
> because apart from me you can do nothing.
>
> JOHN 15:5

CELEBRATING AND OWNING THE NAME

When the name has been chosen, a simple celebration could take place to help members own their new identity. Elements may include the following:

ENVIRONMENT

A picture or icon of the saint may be placed in a prominent place with a candle or flowers near it.

SONG

Choose an appropriate song that pertains to the patron or includes the words of the aspect of Scripture included in the name.

PRAYER

Select a favorite prayer to the saint or write a prayer that emphasizes the reason for the chosen name.

READING

Choose a passage from Scripture, a reading from the writings of the saint, or a passage from the life of the saint.

RITUAL

Create a simple ritual. For example, if "Salt of the Earth" is chosen as a name, each person may take and eat a small amount of salt. If "The Spirit of God" is chosen, the gifts of the Holy Spirit can be printed on small pieces of paper cut into the form of flames and each person can choose one as a gift they will pray for that year.

SHARING

Invite each person to affirm the name by saying why they agree to the name chosen or to name the quality of the saint they most admire.

CLOSING PRAYER

Conclude with spontaneous intercessory prayer, the Lord's Prayer, and a celebratory song.

FESTIVE FOOD

Simple festive food suitable to the culture of the community may be served to continue the celebration.

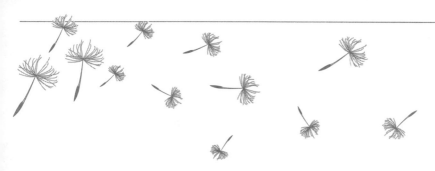

A SAMPLE COMMITMENT FOR SMALL COMMUNITIES

During the first meeting, the small community leader encourages participants to agree on certain principles to facilitate the process of faith sharing. These statements can be distributed at the second meeting as a reminder to all. Below is a sample small Christian community commitment.

THE SOWERS' COMMITMENT

As a small Christian community, we agree

1. *to meet every Tuesday evening from 7:30 to 9:00 PM and to begin and end on time*

2. *to read the materials beforehand*

3. *to hold in confidence what others say*

4. *to share with honesty and openness*

5. *to allow others to speak first before speaking a second time*

6. *to be comfortable with silence*

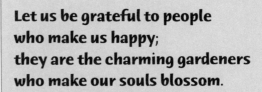

Let us be grateful to people who make us happy; they are the charming gardeners who make our souls blossom.

MARCEL PROUST

7. *to use "I" language whenever possible*

8. *to pray for each other during the week*

9. *to evaluate the experience after six weeks*

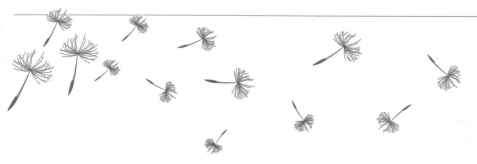

SMALL CHRISTIAN COMMUNITY COVENANTS

Members of some small Christian communities may choose to express their commitment to one another by writing a group covenant. A covenant is simply an agreement in which the members formalize their intention of how they wish to be a small Christian community. It may include their name, purpose, how, when, and where they will meet, how they will handle conflicts, new members, members who decide to leave, how they will celebrate, how they will connect to the wider Church, their communal mission, and other areas deemed important to the community members.

It takes prayer, intense listening to each other, and usually a good facilitator to help the community reach agreement on each area. When the covenant is completed and all agree to their ownership of it, it may be typed or printed, and signed by each person. A prayerful celebration followed by a social would be in order. Perhaps

All the flowers of all the tomorrows are in the seeds of today.

AUTHOR UNKNOWN

the covenant is framed, brought to each meeting, and placed in a prominent place as a reminder to all of their mutual commitment. Or it may be duplicated and given to each member as a constant inspiration of who the community is and the commitments the group has made. It can also serve as a reminder to pray for each member. It may also be read periodically at a small community gathering, especially when key decisions are made or conflicts arise. (For more on writing a covenant, see *Getting a Grip on Your Group*, by Barbara Darling, Good Ground Press, 2002.)

What kinds of small church communities might decide to write a covenant? Those *small Christian communities* who have met in an ongoing way for a period of time and have the desire and commitment to continue to meet together may decide to formalize their intention and write a covenant statement. On campus, we suggest that even semester groups covenant with one another. The members realize they have grown in friendship with each other, grown in deeper relationship with God, and are engaged in individual or common outreach. They desire to make a deeper commitment to God, to one another, and to the world.

Some small communities that start out as *seasonal small groups* (that is, for six weeks in Lent and in the fall) continue to meet seasonally at least twice a year and perhaps periodically between seasons. Their members may feel they are really a small Christian community and may decide to write a covenant. Why? Although they do not meet in an ongoing way, they feel bonded to one another; they are committed to one another; they pray daily for each other; they gather for special occasions, for example, at a family picnic each summer; and do other outreach activities together during the year.

The two types of community given above and others such as intentional communities with a particular focus or intergenerational communities may also decide to write covenants.

RENEW International has always proclaimed that it is God who builds community. We, as staff, simply plant seeds, offer formation, resources, and support. We have never decided which communities are small Christian communities, but have noted that when small communities incorporate the five elements of prayer, faith sharing, mutual support, ongoing learning, and outreach into their lives, they are well on their way to becoming small Christian communities.

In the chapter entitled "FAQs of Small Community Leaders," we gave a working definition of a small Christian community (see page 1). For the sake of clarity, it is repeated here:

> A Christian community is a group of people who are bonded by and strive to live by Jesus' vision and values. A small Christian community or a small church community is a group of people who come together in an ongoing way within the Christian tradition to pray, to reflect on a passage of Scripture, to share their life stories in light of the Word, and then to commit to live out the Word in their daily lives. Another way of saying this might be: a group of people committed to one another, to God, and to the world who desire the gospel to touch every aspect of their lives.

Small Christian communities are not determined by frequency of meetings, but by the genuineness and consistency of members' commitments.

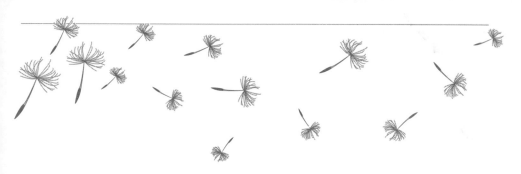

A MEDITATION
FOR SOWERS

It helps, now and then, to step back and take a long view.
The Kingdom of God is not only beyond our efforts,
it is even beyond our vision.

We accomplish in our lifetime only a tiny fraction
of the magnificent enterprise
that is God's work.

Nothing we do is complete,
which is a way of saying that the Kingdom
always lies beyond us.

No statement says all that could be said.
No prayer fully expresses our faith.
No confession brings perfection,
no pastoral visit brings wholeness.
No program accomplishes the Church's mission.
No set of goals and objectives includes everything.

This is what we are about:
We plant the seeds that one day will grow.
We water seeds already planted,
knowing that they hold future promise.
We lay foundations that will need further development.
We provide yeast that produces effects
far beyond our capabilities.

We cannot do everything,
and there is a sense of liberation in realizing that.
This enables us to do something,
and to do it very well.

It may be incomplete,
but it is a beginning,
a step along the way,
an opportunity for the Lord's grace
to enter and do the rest.

We may never see the end results,
but that is the difference
between the master builder and the worker.

We are workers, not master builders,
ministers, not messiahs.
We are prophets of a future that is not our own.

According to Msgr. John P. Zenz, Moderator of the Curia and Vicar General
of the Archdiocese of Detroit, Cardinal John Dearden included this poetic
reflection in a homily given on October 25, 1979 at Blessed Sacrament
Cathedral, Detroit. Often mistakenly ascribed to Archbishop Oscar Romero,
it most likely was authored by Father Ken Untener (later bishop of Saginaw)
when he worked with Cardinal Dearden in Detroit.

Seasonal Small Community Member Evaluation

After completing this evaluation, share one way God has touched you through this community and celebrate it with spontaneous prayer and light refreshments.

Name some situations when you felt the most energy coming from your small community.

What has happened this Season in your community that has had the most impact on you? Why?

In what ways is belonging to a small Christian community important to you?

How has your faith sharing challenged you to live out the gospel in a new way this Season?

What suggestions might you have for your facilitator to help improve your community's time together?

From *Sowing Seeds: Essentials for Small Community Leaders* © 2008 RENEW International

Seasonal Small Community
Leader Evaluation

Name some situations when you felt the most energy coming from your small community.

In what ways have you seen your members grow together in becoming community?

What indications do you see in your members (or what feedback have they given) that show this faith-sharing experience has impacted their lives?

In what ways has your small community demonstrated a commitment to living the gospel? (How have they reached out? What impact did they have?)

What suggestions do you have to improve their time together?

What wisdom or understanding did you gain from your experience as leader? How will this impact how you fulfill your role in the future?

From *Sowing Seeds: Essentials for Small Community Leaders* © 2008 RENEW International

RESOURCES

IMPACT Series and Observe, Judge, Act

RENEW International publishes the IMPACT Series for small communities. This series aims to connect faith to a wide range of human concerns and personal issues. In the process, participants will not only be led to prayerful reflection and fruitful sharing, but also to concrete actions that influence attitudes and behaviors. Growth through action is a basic principle in the IMPACT Series. In addition to encouraging discussion and sharing, this series leads to concrete action.

Published materials like *Reflections on Dead Man Walking* or *Finding God at Work* can bring issues or circumstances of the present day right into our lives and force us to think about what is happening in our world and in our everyday lives. While many of us may rather not be challenged in this way, using such titles from the IMPACT Series is another manner in which we are being called to understand the gospel and, perhaps, to follow Jesus' call.

Some of the IMPACT Series materials that deal with social issues use the **Observe>Judge>Act** methodology because of its proven ability to lead to thoughtful and effective action. When using the **Observe>Judge>Act** methodology, it is suggested that two or three weeks intervene between group sessions, thus allowing members of the community time to act and make further observations in preparation for the upcoming meeting.

Many issues are somewhat difficult to face and to grasp. Experience shows that such issues are seldom addressed without a certain amount of challenge, guidance, and assistance. All titles in the IMPACT Series are designed to meet this need and, in doing so, to help small Christian communities realize better their great potential for ushering in the fullness of God's reign on Earth.

Prayer

Two popular IMPACT Series titles on prayer are *At Prayer with Mary* (6 sessions) and *Awakening the Mystic Within* (6 sessions).

Christian Prayer: Deepening My Experience of God (12 sessions), part of the *Why Catholic? Journey through the Catechism* Series, is an excellent resource that offers reflections on prayer, how God communicates with us, different forms of prayer, some difficulties we experience in prayer, as well as a deeper look at the Lord's Prayer. The book uses various styles of prayer in the sessions. For additional information on the above titles, please visit www.renewintl.org/store

Immersion Experience

Immersion experiences were mentioned in the chapter, "Leaven for Transforming the World." For more information on an immersion experience, contact Cuernavaca Center for Intercultural Dialog and Development (CCIDD). The Center's mission is to provide opportunities for churches and other groups from the United States and Canada to encounter the presence of God in the struggle for justice in the Americas and to empower them to work for social transformation.

Cuernavaca Center for Intercultural Dialog and Development
Francisco Layva 39
Cuernavaca, Morelos
62000 Mexico

Send correspondence to:
Cuernavaca Center for Intercultural Dialog and Development
413 Interamericana Blvd. WH1
PMB 21-63
Laredo, TX 78045

Phone: (011-52-777) 312-65-64
USA line direct to Mexico : 414-431-4244
Fax: (011-52-777) 312-93-92
Email: ccidd@cableonline.com.mx
Website: www.ccidd.org